Summer in the virus's shadow

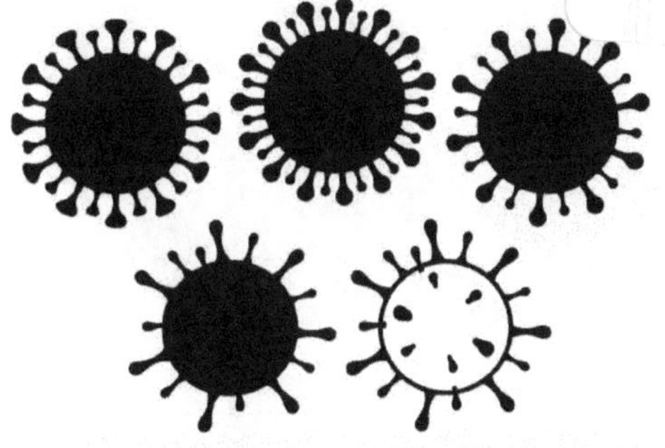

Jan Oskar Hansen

The Author

Jan Oskar Hansen is a poet, story teller and seafarer, born in Stavanger, Norway. He joined the merchant navy at 15 and spent most of his life at sea until settling in the early 90's in Portugal. His poetry has been widely published in hard copy and online, worldwide. Reviewers have generally commented that a love and honoring of living things stands out in Hansen's work, and deep humility; that it reveals with unflinching honesty man's shortcomings in his efforts to love, telling what there is to tell in a first person, deeply resident universal voice.

The poet is widely read and fluent in several languages, knowledge often acquired at night during his many years at sea. He chose to write primarily in English following enthusiastic reception of his work from English-speaking editors and readers. His poems have been published in over 20 literary magazines worldwide, including:

Hudson Review, USA, Skyline, USA, Skald, Wales, La rue Bella, England, The Bards, England, War is a dangerous place, England, The Black Mountain Review, Ireland, ARS Poetica India, India, Metvere Muse, India, Poets International, India, Braquemard, England, Fvirefly Magazine, USA, Pphoo, India, Taj Mahal Review, India, Remark Magazine, USA, Journal Of Anglo-Scandianvian Poetry, England.

His poems appeared in the following anthologies:

Shaken & Stirred (Bewrite Books, UK, 2003), Routes – Twelve Poets (Bewrite Books, UK, 2004), A Road Less Traveled (Bewrite Books, UK, 2005), Poetry from the Far Corners (Bewrite Books, UK, 2005), Listening to the birth of crystal (Paulapublishing, 2004) England, Peoplespoet 2 (Paulapublishing, 2005) England, The Review of contemporary poetry (Bluechrome, 2005) England, The book of hopes and dreams (Bluechrome, 2006) England.

Collections "Letters from Portugal" (bewrite books) Bristol, "La Strada" (Lapwing publishers) Belfast, "End of Voyage" (WFP. New York), "Marilyn Monroe remembered" Erbacce Press. Liverpool, "The Fairground" Ranchi India (out of print now).

Contents

Wishful thinking

I can meet you in an open field
or a place where bombs fall I shall be prepared
there is no one to blame but life itself
so quickly taken away like a switch on my lamp
or failing breaks in my ca. I have a secret weapon
my memory will stretch until infinity
it encompasses the galaxy and beyond because
I remember my birth and the stone age.
nothing is forgotten, my brain is a computer
stores everything from the banal to the sublime
from here to there in a blink of an eye, you shall
not defeat me.

....

shame on you

I was about eighteen when meeting the girl of my life,
she lived in the outer town and both her parents had office work
which back then was regarded as a posh position.
We met often walked in the park, and we kissed chastely hold
hands, this was love.
It was a pleasant Saturday even when she came she scented
of wild roses how beautiful she was, we went to a restaurant
we sat there as long as we could, it worried me to take her home
I lived in my mothers tiny flat.
There was no welcome. My mother stayed in her bedroom
I told the girl she wasn´t well.
We sat on the sofa the one I used as a bed, as it was chilly we
sat covered in a blanket until we both fell asleep.
There was no bathroom, only cold water from the tap in
the kitchen and we walked to town to the railway station where

she had a wash and the rest.
We didn't speak about the night spent together, sat silently
on a bench, waiting for the train to take her home.
When she boarded the train, there was no talk of meeting again,

only a short goodbye and she was out of my life.

----

the journey home

It´s time to go home to the village where I belong
in Algarve where everyone knows my name
and tourists are a rare sight.
I have to drive across the Alentejo, and it is too hot
I have to wait for September when begin to cool down
so I can stop and take in the sight of galloping horses
who run for the fun of it and donkeys slowly
pulling carts not to forget the sheep resting under
a tree in the peace that only happens to the holy.
I will take the long road home. The motorway is like
driving in a roofless tunnel.
If the journey is too long, I stay a night at a small hotel
have good farmers breakfast and carry on there is no
rush the dwelling will be there waiting patiently
for me to keep it company

....

The plague

s

been a virus spike near us
an actress died there was a picture of her
on the news when she received a prize,
she had scarf flung around her shoulder

expensive only
for festive occasions and meeting the minister
of culture.
The virus is like the dust that flows on the road
it changes direction many times and might hit you.
The pestilence will disappear one the day they say.
I don´t think so, where is it supposed to go
hiding in a cave or buried under the soil.
Perhaps we should stop eating jungle meat
or any meat, I´m thinking of chicken farming that is so unspeak-
able cruel we deserve what we get.
So, we wear masks only because it gives us the illusion of safety,

and the chance will do the rest.

When it rains

I look through my window at the star on the night sky
without them, it would have been like being blind
and I would have to look at the petrol station up the road
it is painted green and is not a wonder of architect wonder.
Sometimes rain heavy clouds block the stars,
I like rain it is needed, but not when it falls on me.
I walked in a night forest in the rain, looking for a lake that
has an inner glow from there I could find my way home
as the battery of my flashlight had gone.
I know what the animals snug in their burrows was thinking
what is this thundering fool doing here? A rabbit said he is looking
for a lake

to cure his heartache. We can understand
that a fox said hadn´t it been raining I would have guided him

with that the other animals fell about laughing.

Pluto, the forgotten planet

Mars is a stony planet, too big for its own good
those who go there have to live indoors as it has no air to breath
life for the brave must be tedious looking a reddish stones
and the occasionally a yellow dust storm is living up.
One by one the will commit suicide venturing out and explode.
Pluto, on the other hand is a small planet and it has green vegetation.
A place to grow potatoes and cabbage
it has fruit too not like
here on earth but nevertheless they are tasty
except for the blue lemon that is poisonous
The fauna is full of odd-looking animals that are so friendly
no one wants to kill them becoming vegetarians instead.
Take the enormous flightless fowl they lay eggs that can serve
a battalion for breakfast. There is no tobacco
on the planet but it has big leaves which
when rolled together makes people happy and laughing, on earth
we call it marijuana an odd name for a delicate plant.
There is no snow on Pluto, no clouds but the sun can be
a little off-putting as it is smoky brow.
So why is no one going there, say, on holiday for later to live
there permanently, but forget your snowboard and skis.

----

the milking cows

cows originally had small udders after all
they had milk for a calf and when needed could run very fast
quicker than a man.
They were hunted like we hunt elk today, until someone
hungry tried to drink its milk and found it nourishing.
It was a eureka moment, and we domesticated the cow.
The bigger the udder, the better the cow.
It is not natural to see a cow with enormous udder they
is a freak of nature but highly regarded by the milk industry
and look comical when trying to run.
The big udder has passed over to the way we view women
a big breasted woman is admired.
We don´t need so much milk anymore there are alternative
to milk by using plant-based products to make cheese and
yoghurts, it is time to let the cow be normal again

Mermaids in a lake

It is hot today I try to write
words are like wet cement in a ditch
covering empty cola cans thrown from cars
by careless drivers who care not for nature.
ABC full stop.
I stood by the entrance in the shade someone
asked if I was the porter, I smiled benignly
didn´t get upset after all I´m working class.
Had they asked me if I was the director
I might have been less inclined to smile.
I miss my home it is near a forest with a lake
mermaids swim there and have proper feet.
Once I swam with them a dream come true
when it is winter, and the lake is like an ice rink
I skate around and around until I get dizzy and fall

into a trance the dream of mermaids
revive me. I walk home in silence.

,,,,,,,,,,,

The love impossible

The cafe was full, a young woman
was looking for a table, I told her to sit at mine,
she did, she was Irish and, yes, had green eyes
and I fell instantly in love.
We exchanged phone numbers I rang her the next day
her phone was disconnected, she never rang me.
I was devastated felt as fate had robbed me taken my true love away,

and the five children we
would have had. (had given them names)
if I remember right, she wore a sheepskin coat and an emerald ring,

I wonder if she still has the ring?

the young are the future

What worries me although I will not live in the future
is the young people those with little education no prospect
beginning their life as losers.
We and the police of money are to blame they were not
in our mind forgotten in the miasma of big-city poverty.
The young form bands it gives them a sense of belonging
defending their turf and knives sit loosely in the sheath.
I believe we need a political party free of class, an abomination
race and creed, a society that is all-inclusive and open for all
in short a benign system.
Will we get this utopia for the next generation, I fear not
but when a few survivors of the looming disaster sit
on the shores of Himalaya fishing for mackerel we may get there
providing there is no dispute about fishing rights.

Memories and a farm

My mother had tuberculosis and sent to a sanatorium
I ended up in a home run by the local town and financed
by people who meant well
I made life difficult for the staff, and a tiny boy went on strike
they sent me to a farm, back then farmers were paid
by the community taking children from poor homes.
For me, it was a beautiful place, the farmer and his wife were
a middle-aged couple and the demanded little of me except
getting up early milking the cows, they had five.
I have always liked animals and domestic animals
they had no reason to fear me.
The school was an hour walk away if I crossed the fields
it got shorter when I got a bike.
Years went by. My mother was coming back, although
she had only a small flat, and I had to sleep on the floor
I loved her and left the idyllic farm to memories.

Facebook

serious writing is not suited in Facebook
and if you are political and write about the atrocity of Israel
there is silence no one says a word it is like farting in church.
Philosophy is a waste of time levity is the norm.
The truth of our lives and days is packed in like a joke.
Infantile writing about girls is OK providing the lust is hidden
and we get served banalities, cute children and flowers.
I know this, the silence and lack of serious debate, people
don´t want to know before the calamity of reality hits them
But I keep sending in stuff to Facebook and twitter where
I am listened to with agreement or anger.
I write in the Facebook in the hope someone will say fuck off
a proof that I have stirred someone into action.

Robots at sea

the sun shines, it always shines, on the portholes
on the ships in the bay looking enticing.
To be a mariner is not a natural form of life and
should be run by robots can tie a ship to a port.
As it is an engineer can sit in a control room
and press the relevant buttons no need for an oiler
to walk around seeing if something has to be done
and cleaning the floor.
On long journeys by the young especially is not
healthy, too much time spent reading pornography
and getting a wrong view of what sex is.
Visiting prostitutes thinking women are like this.
Come to think of it robots could be used as soldiers
and the interest in armies would lessen.

The Dolphin and I

I think it was in 1967 when the Junta of Greek coronels
took power, I was in Piraeus on holiday
the water on the stretch is calm, and one day I met a dolphin
we swam side by side and when I got tired I hold around
her she was helping me ashore.
We had a platonic affair kissing and cuddling like lovers
beautiful days and she was always there waiting for me.
It came to an abrupt end when one evening I criticized
the junta which consist of four rather dim officers and
for good measure had a go at the Orthodox priests,

who looked like they were eating a cow a day.
I blame the ouzo.
I had been overheard and the police. came drove me
to the airport and there was no time to say goodbye.
It must have been disheartening for the dolphin it must
have waited for a day, we were lovers torn apart by politic.
There was another coup, and the colonels were exiled to an

an island that had an asylum were, they became orderlies
which they liked so much that when they were forgiven
stayed on because the mad did as they were told.
But I cannot forgive them for destroying a beautiful love story

----

Haiku riddle

tons of garbage
left by those who want peace
the right to be shitty

people like to march
to the tune of pied piper
social conscience

when everyone concurs
they are usually dead wrong
bombs are exploding

consensus are fakes
foisted on naive people
thinking in unison

beware of peace traders
they want you to agree with them
dark hearts of hate

Life as we know it

I think we humans suffer from a death wish
we destroy nature, a heatwave in Siberia
burning down down the Amazon all in day´s work.
After this pandemic, the next one will be worse
we may be the last humans before we go up inflames

tempted throw off my mask, kiss people
and mingle with the crowd.
Apart from wearing the mask, I'm into hugging strangers,

but I can change.
Yet, there is always a yet, life is the only thing
we know, death is a foreign existence we now little
about and we fear its appearing nothingness.

----

the tragedy of 1948

Israel declared statehood the west was happy
the Jews had suffered much and deserved a state
the fact that 700 thousand Palestinians lost
their homeland was overlooked.
We were all pro- Israel back then and thought
the region would usher in peace and prosperity.
It was not to be.
Instead, we see that the land of promise has
turned violent wanting all of Palestine and part of Syria
and Jordan too, they appear unstoppable.
The only group holding them back a little is the Hezbollah
who we call a terrorist, but they are a bulwark
the brutal regime in Israel who has nothing to offer but
a war against anyone opposing their quest for total power.
But the Palestinians are not forgotten the scale fell
from our eyes, we see what is happening.
Israel as a state should be boycotted, we in the west
should treat the country as an abomination it is.
By curtailing Israel, we will, in the long run, help its survival.
Force it back to the agreed borders, declare Palestine
a sovereign state, and send NATO troops to secure the perimeter
of Palestine and give financial help to her malign people.

So, the party is over

from Rushmore no soothing words
of a nation coming together
to overcome the virus that kills so many
all we got was more hate and division
and people sans mask applauding.
In Germany, people were fervent admirers
of Hitler, we didn´t understand why
despite his anti-Semitic rants, yet the people
clung to his Nazism to the end.
Like a virus, the unbecoming philosophy
spread to Israel, the victims this time are
the Palestinians and the passive world looks
on doing nothing to stop this madness.
We live in a world of denial where truth is
not of interest, but lies are the common currency
repeated by the press endlessly.
I look out of the window it is Sunday morning
it pains me I can do nothing to stop this
cauldron we live in from boiling over.

The brain

It is more difficult now
the ready wit and one-liners sound laborious
there has been a decline
realism taking over you are not going anywhere
does it matter?
Trying to write soberly but with a tiny smile
it is easier to accept things as they are
get along a friend of everyone, an unblushing lie
I tell you a secret, the restriction on assembly
suits me fine I suffer from a mild form of agoraphobia
and are quite nervous in public, now the excuse
is perfect I can stay put.
It is hard to write words no longer pops up I have
to go looking for them and they are grumpy when
awoken and put to use.
So, I accept the thing as being what it is for now.

The Patient

My wife and I are old
she has a brother who is very ill and leaves
the hospital in a few days
well, we cannot leave him in a dingy hotel.
I do not think we should be burdened
with a very sick person, not at our age, but things
are what they are so he is welcome.
We have arranged for a woman/nurse to come
in the morning to wash him and so on
so that will be OK.
I suspect what his illness consist of, but can´t
tell my wife and upset her.
We are giving my wife´s brother a beautiful room and
his bathroom, and then we wait...

the malefactor

I had a thieving dog
she stole eggs, one at the time
kept it in her mouth she wanted to give it to me.
I took the egg, just as the hen-lady came
screaming said the dog and I worked in tandem.
I gave the lady back her egg
she refused to take it, not surprising,
so I paid for the egg.
A dog doesn´t know human morality it has to be thought
to leave the neighbours thing alone.

Art centre

At Louvre tourists are taking selfies
in the background a painting of someone famous
it doesn't matter who it is as long as the label
"fame" is stuck to it.
It is self-regarding they see themselves through
the lenses and never mind the statue of
someone called Rodan; they are not sure.
They send their badly taken picture to friends
who more than likely delete this because they
need a place for their own selfies.
Art is seen through cell phones, something
fuzzy on a wall.

The modern world

Strange times we live
experience
is virtual
the real is harmful
bad for the health.
The internet gives us link
but our solitude
is the same.
Famous women
do not look factual
like something made in a factory
we tend to be self-absorbed
our feeling and thoughts
are truncated
into a massive none entity
stalking the world
while polar ice melt
and we can cross the seas
on plastic bottles
as seen on the internet
and therefore appears unreal

Absent-minded

The light was on in every room
she was up but still asleep, sat in the kitchen
watching a blank TV screen.
I gently squeezed her shoulder, starlet she woke up
said, I must have fallen asleep.
Going back to bed, she scolded me for not switching
off the light.
I said nothing looking for my reading glasses, which
I found in the fridge beside forbidden chocolate,
two tomatoes, lettuce and a half-eaten apple.

Suggestible me

I had ended up in a country with a strange pub culture
and obsession with the class which I found restrictive.
No posh pubs if the working class and not slumming it
if you were middle class, and the rich lived in Bermuda.
I was full of terror and uncertainty this world was
not of my liking to get through the day I drank a lot
mainly at home or in the park.
My new wife said I was an alcoholic and a nice man
from AA came and took me to a meeting where people
sat around a table talking about themselves and how much
they had suffered, while I am just getting out, was a full
of the terror of agoraphobia.
I suddenly had many friends, but they were mates only
as long as I went to their meeting, that over time became
repetitive like reading the same book a hundred times.
I stopped going to their gatherings went to the library instead
and spent happy days reading, but lost my friends.
Finally, after a nervous breakdown, I got much help from
a psychologist to confront my fears.
But I was never at ease in this country I left and is blessed
in Portugal where no one knows my name.

Mass Immigration

Once upon a time, there was a mass emigration
from Northern Europe to America, caused by social injustice
and bitter poverty.
46%n of the population in Norway immigrated to the USA,
the immigrants settled mainly in places like Minnesota and
another northern state as farmers as the land was easy to come
by.
Few of them came back to Norway, those who did were
to show off their wealth such as a big car,
having a car was beyond reach for ordinary people even up to
the ninety fifties.
No sane Scandinavian goes to America anymore, this because
politically the USA didn´t evolve but in many ways regressed
into boneheaded conservationism.
Yet for many, say, Latin America where people have suffered
under various dictatorships, North America still offers hope
of work and food on the table.

The unspoken

The tall deep green grass on the plateau
is undulating ominously today as an unseen virus
is formed and breathes down the valley.
Reindeer´s bones are a signal of things to come
the silence of mass- graves is menacing.
Thresholds are defenseless keeping the pestilence
from entering your rooms killing the fire
in your heart and apathy rots from the inside.
Ice cold is the blues sky it will not yield,
the deep green grass whisper there is no escape
join us now.

Where the sea is deep

As he sank into the deep sea, he became
pellucid, familiar fish ignored him so did unsightly shrimps
the insect of the sea.

As he sank deeper, there was less life but the life that existed
was strange and ghostly grotesque forms ugly for untrained
eye, yet the not ungainly.

A ship sank in deep water it was 1944, and a war raged,
her captain was still on the bridge giving a command to
the third officer ho had lost his uniform showing his skeletal body

The captain´s dislike this display proper dressed on my bridge
he used to say, and clean fingernails are a must as important
as wearing proper shoes.

The rest of the crew on the ship had gone walkabout and
found they liked this new world, much better than the war
fought on the surface of the sea.

He discovered funnels of whirling air, entered one and was
shot to the surface and a wave washed him ashore
on a pristine beach that soon would be a war scene-

Tomorrow

thorny bushes
ripped t. shirt
dripping blood
stopped, which way to go
forward, the bushes
must thin out
upfront
and reveal a landscape
of bliss.
Retreat
back to the beginning
that is painful too.
It is good to know
when losing-
there is tomorrow

Palm oil

when one writes about minorities
no one wants to know, the next page about knitting, please.
We do not like to read about losers
and our responsibility for their failure.
A tsunami came rolled over the landscape, changed it
and the language, unstoppable misery for the people
who lived there, but it brought us the automobile.
The Palestinians have lost most of their land and now
they are losing more, except their dignity.
We don´t want to know, the next page about knitting, please.
Let us read about the super-rich, their yachts
and Rolls Royce, we like to see the pictures of them
in magazines, their villas and life mode
we dislike the truth, and it demands us to sit up straight
and think about the world and the orangutan losing
their habitat to palm oil.

The great change

I have a mask made of plastic glass covers the whole
face to avoid touching my face, of the type dogs, were
not to scratch their ears.
Surgical gloves are must when going to the shop, there
is nowhere else to go.
I don't think the virus is going away this year or next
we have to ignore it and walk in the park.
Go to the beach swim a little and sit in the warm sand
drinking a beer and hotly kiss a girl.
Either that or sit naked on the terrace waving my cock around
no that it will scare anyone, fart and pee into the town.
I can sing "they are coming to take me away" until the police
knock down the door and take me away.
A smooth cell and no bloody mask "are you feeling better."
Aa white-coated man asks, they now I'm diabetic and prone
to an angry outburst, but he has a needle for that.
Once there was a law not hiding your face in public, now
It is the other way around.
Many things have changed the padre stand in an empty
Church, there is not an alter boys to seduce, he lifts
up his cassock and masturbate in front of the statue of Christ.

Green wave

I wish I were a green wave in the south Atlantic crash on the
shores of Newfound land, walk up a steep hill and down on the
other side.
Find a village and get lamb with mint sauce.
Then, I will be back to the sea, swim among icebergs, sit on a floe
dressed in a polar- bear coat and think of Sweden.
I country that killed everyone over fifty as a deliberate policy
to give room for Pakistani and their prayer mats.
The idea was a new, young workforce, but what they get are people
who congregate in towns only speak their language and take
no Interest in Sweden which they regard as a Christian county.
Where they live, they will enforce the Shari law and chopping off
heads. all that is needed now a black sword across the Swedish
flag
and the battle is won

Hormones

in the old days, ships were harder to handle and needed
a crew of about 32 people, modern ships need a team of 6 or seven
they had mess-boys back then our jobs were to serve food
do the washing up. We were very, young about 15 to 16 years old
and hormones were flying about making trouble.
Sometimes we met in a cabin for communal masturbation to see
how long we could keep it from exploding.
Once I hit the ceiling with my sperm and won kudos for this effort.
On long voyages we often fought, the slightest word
often led to a fistfight; I usually had a nosebleed
shorter trips were more natural, the dockland was full of whores who
liked us because we were young smelling youth and innocence
which we relied on for a free fuck.
But our innocence disappeared, and we had to pay like everybody else.
I had the luck to join a ship trading along ports in Latin America
were women were virtually free of charge, a promise to write was
often
sufficient, their dream Europe and away from poverty.
As I got older and more aware of my surrounding, I had been a part
of exploitation, and since I became a socialist, I preached my new
found
to ears that would not hear.

indoors

since people outside wear masks
and I can´t see if they laugh or cry.
Since bars are shut.
Since I´m reduced to look at ladies handbags
in the posh nearby
there is little point going out.

The month of birth

The month of the year when born
does matter
My brother was born in June
and sunlight followed him all his days.
And friend he had many warming
their meagre souls in his light.
I was born a mournful October morning
the sky cried, and the nurse said
he has an old soul.
In my presence, people tend to go away gloomy
and moderate my opinion.
Rain does not stop for happiness
and a wish I will shut up.
I have a few friends wish I had more, but October
is not so forgiving

Sunday morning

I like to go home
to the village in the mountain
and the dog that loved me unreservedly
but she wanted to reinforce our bond
stroking her head whispering sweet words
I like to look back a whole lifetime for a dog
she was proud of me, a couple for a stroll
through her life.
Looking back I think this was my best moment
the creation of true friendship.

love is forever

I had an aunt who fell in love with a soldier
their home was an oasis in a restless time, and they had a child.
Her and his love were resolute nothing could separate them.
How wrong and naive they were, he was called to serve at
the Russian front, he pleaded with the officer to let him see
the war out with his beloved, but an order was an order.
My aunt never saw him again he disappeared in the churning
steppe machinery.
When peace came she suffered much abuse, people calling
her a tart to use a friendly word
she never married again was steadfast in her love for him
and cherished the time they had together.
Sometimes love fall where it falls there is no consideration
like confetti strewn in the air.
She had fallen in love with a German soldier and had to pay
a heavy toll-

from a day

Remember there a good time when we thought "Reader's digest.
Was high literature, the teller of the truth?
When I was propagandist luring us with fine luring us
in lies.
When we got older we learned and these days even the Guardian
follows a political policy skirting the truth.
There are the lie and the truth, but convention stops us from telling
anyone how it was.
I wrote a story of sea life and young men the story was met
pith d deadly silence because I used the language of a time gone
when a whore was not a sex-worker.
People feel offended when met with untarnished truth,
write about the green sea and not of mass- murder of old people
in Sweden.
An editor wrote me a long letter of refusal when to simple
words like "fuck off "would be better and less insulting.
But that is the way it is better to be kind than truthful.

A sober revenge

there is on the plateau of Spain a town made of yellow bricks
the buildings are of the same size, seven floors and on top an artist
studio.
The street bellow was narrow had many bars and shops selling socks
it can get cold in Spain too.
On the fourth floor, in one of the building, lived a couple. He had a drink
the problem and she scolded him for this but since he said sorry-looking
contrite
she forgave him and made him a tortilla.
Then it so happened he stopped drinking altogether
and he took over the economic side of the household.
She took to placing bottles around the flat, but to a no awhile he the
husband, A sober revenge.
There is on the plateau of Spain a town made of yellow bricks
the buildings are of the same size, seven floors and on top an artist studio.
The street bellow was narrow had many bars and shops selling socks
it can get cold in Spain too.
On the fourth floor, in one of the building, lived a couple. He had a drink
the problem and she scolded him for this but since he said sorry-looking
contrite
she forgave him and made him a tortilla.
Then it so happened he stopped drinking altogether
and he took over the economic side of the household.
She took to placing bottles around the flat, but to a no awhile he
the husband, stayed sober, and she felt relegated.
With little to do, she got hold of a small restaurant in the base-
ment. Lovely though the man now I can come and get my lunch
every day.

His wife resented this. He was taking up a table eating up the profit, so, he was refused a meal.
Undaunted he had his lunch at another cafe and when asked why he was eating
there and not at his wife´s place,
he said, my wife, is not a good cook!
Now there are many empty tables at her restaurant during lunch

The Lady from Lisbon

I corresponded with a lady from Lisbon
one day she came to see me carrying a small suitcase
and wine cooler, the cooler was surprised she never drank.
When we went to bed at night, she said she had the menstruation
OK., for me, sex is not everything.
Later she said had been joking, but in the night I felt as I had
blood in my mouth.
After breakfast, she said she had to visit a friend,
and off she went with her small suitcase and wine cooler.
She promised to ring me, never did, which I was glad to hear this.
This is a strange country, rice cooked in chicken blood,
coked ox ball in thick brown gravy.
They also serve sliced blood sausages, needless to say
I avoid food with blood.

The booze

I always have been a drinker. My first wife divorced me
citing my drinking, but of course, she was English.
My Portuguese wife has a more relaxed attitude to booze
but now my doctor has taken the key to the drinks cabinet
and throw it into the bay.
My mind went on lockdown
when I try to write it appears wooden and trite, it is like
the sober me is too critical of self and others.
A cold beer at six in the afternoon is out so is the evening wine
that inspired me to write that my befuddled brain was happy
to read.
The other day I upset a friend of mine, it appears I had hit a sore
point.
My remarks, if tame, nevertheless was unnecessary.
Life on the sober lane is cumbersome and stony
so, I will end my writing and lat the glorious past speak for me.

Like a painting

Is anything more beautiful than an early morning
in Cheshire, I walked along a lone it was like being
in the middle of a painting dripping leaves and
dew on the grass.
A lone horse came to the fence I stroked it. Then
it went back grazing again no longer alone.
On the other side of the field a gate opened., a flock
of sheep came, company good enough for the horse
I was free to go.

The fox in the hen house

The settlers are burning down Palestinians olive tree,
No main newspapers care to report the truth the settlers are
conniving.
With the Israeli government to do this unopposed.
What we a witnessing is the destruction of a people who had
their land was stolen and hounded to elimination by those who chose
to believe what a scribe said.
There have been many massacres over time like what happened
to the Albanians and other minorities such as the Rohingya people
In the hands of the Buddhists.
We have had the Holocaust, but it is the first time we are seeing
The oppressed are becoming oppressors, and they are so successful
That if we protest, they are calling us anti- Semitic.

he heartland

When Carl Was about twenty-two yours old, tall and handsome
with slight gay air, many women liked he decided to open
a refined massage saloon.
It took time before the place got going he borrowed from me
which he repaid handsomely when his business established.
But he got bored with the work oiling fat thigh and let his hands
inside smelling vaginas and softly massage the clitoris
until they relaxed. Happy for a few hours.
Carl Hired an assistant a "Dr Fred" he looked like a man a woman
would have as a lover, and his mien there was a half promise
that someday somewhere it would come to fruition.
He bought out Carl for a price under its value, but Carl was happy
he liked nothing better to come into my little bar drinking beer
trying to struggle writing lyric.
Dr Fred committed the cardinal sin: WOME TALK!
He had succumbed to temptation sleeping with a couple of them
it began as a whisper that was loud enough for the paper to hint
that all were not well. The refined saloon was closed down, and
poor Fred got jail time as he was not a doctor.
Men must learn a moral here keep your mouth shut.

The way chosen

They were hopeful
Their son going to university
The furrow they stalked
Came to an abrupt halt.

He ploughed his field
Sometimes over rocky ground
Or stormy seas
Now he looks back contently.

He had walked his way
Not any one's track that leads
To advances and respect
Their sad joy turned to dust.

The Night

The night is asleep over Cascais
I should be asleep too, but many thoughts are keeping me
awake—
a longing for the past.
Tomorrow is Mother's Day. I wrote her a poem
but I'm unable to be sentimental about it,
I should have painted a better picture of her and
strewn rose petals on her path.
that would have been dishonest she was not
a gushy person and insincere words would have
embarrassed her.
It is a beautiful night in Cascais no cold winds are
blowing from the sea rushing around the building
rattling the windows and trying to speak, but it has
no tongue or language.
I like the hot climate like in the Algarve my cottage
is standing there untended and alone
In a night like this, but there is a pandemic like a curse
over the land, and the old are dying.
So, I have to wait till the best is full before going home.

Red Indians

This afternoon was spent watching an old western movie
it was the usual stuff cavalry in spotless uniforms
sitting on tall horses facing a bunch of extras playing
the Indians appeared incredible stupid, were rounded up
and herded back to their dry reservation and poverty.
First time I saw the movie 40 years ago, we laughed a
the Indians they were like a pantomime act how could they
ever rule themselves?
Sometimes I think the Israelis see the Palestinians this way
they have no weapon are reduced throwing stones at soldiers
who no longer care to kill them only knee-cap them.
Dirty Palestinians living in filth, and no think how it came about.
Israel can stop their water supply at a whim.
Oh, those Arabs when are they throwing in the towel and become
quaint people tourists will flock to see.

<<<<<<<<<<dreamy landscape

I followed a narrow track leading up
to the mountain that has a flat, earthy soil.

The dog refused to follow.

On top the sun was hot had a dizzy spell I saw was a patent
donkey
before I fainted.

Someone carried me to a stream with clear water
I drank and found a lump of sugar in my pocket

when I looked around, I saw no one, went to sleep
I used a soft stone as a pillow.

When rested, I walked down on the other side found
a nice bar telling what has happened.

No, no leave the little people alone
we need them more than ever.

They sing for us when nightfall and unafraid
we sleep well and live long.

When coming out of the bar, my dog was waiting
she found a track around the mountain

she led the way looked back to see if I was safe
I had been too long in the bar.

Now I could hear the murmur of their voices so blessed
that dog stop barking.

I slept all night and had no nightmare of a coming war
the scent of thyme seeped down into the valley.

Not a sage

He is old now, and eyes are watery he looks absent
and hiss ready smile has disappeared-
people ask him questions he cannot answer because
he is unwilling to say what they want to hear.
Yes, he is a communist but also critical of its policy
it can so quickly end up with an elite- sham labour unions
and loss of free expressions
Democratic- communism is not possible as people
we have not evolved enough to understand it's the concept
to explain will take too long.
He murmurs something, feigns hard of hearing
and let people talk to each other daily life were everyone
has an opinion, often ill-informed from a sentence
in a respected paper like the Guardian that is political
in a middle-class way.
He knows lies rules the world and that is the way
of our existence.

Time is looking up

Today, for the fist time in month
the restaurant was opening and we had a proper
meal served
by real waiter, although they were obliged
to use masks.
good food on a big table not too man people around
we had a wonderful time with glass of red win.
On Sunday the beaches were full and no one respected
the distance of two meter,
I wasn´t there I dislike walking on sand and the voices
of young people reminded me of a times gone by,
and of course. I do not tolerate sunlight, after skin cancer.
But it was pleasing to get hot food, and too something
served in boxes and left outside, warmed in the micro
still smelling of paper boxes.

inland waterway

I joined the rowing boat in the middle of the dry lake
when a dust storm came whirling around screaming nasty words
and the shoreline disappeared.
The captain came down from the bridge wan ted his lunch
but he had to wait till the wind stopped which it did
in the afternoon.
I walked ashore, at the cafe the knew about the order
the captain had sent a text message.
I eat the food here,I said no point wrapping it up-
Driving home helicopters were using my lake as a training ground
no, there would not be an inland waterway here
no matter how much it rains the lake will only be a soggy hole
but how to explain this to the captain.

The disappearance

The Gulf of Mexico suddenly ran into the Atlantic
left oil rigs high and dry.
Naturally, the USA claimed the land which was disputed
by Mexico and Cuba and Belize.
What was left of the gulf had rivers and lakes
and as the land greened it turned out to be fertile and
the Amish people encouraged to farm the land which they
did with earnest enthusiasm.
Village sprang up, roads were built, and the famous
veterinarian Jan Pol opened up his practice as well.
As years went by, people forgot that they were farming
on what has been the bottom of a sea.
The sea had not forgotten.
Slowly seeping in and those who had built luxury houses
were the first to leave, but the fishery thrived and
the shrimp business had a revival.
There was a mass exodus, and the Amish people went
back farming the land they knew.
When the water had claimed, all of the gulf and people
forgetting. There was only Wikipedia left to give
a brief outline of the past.

Iron horse

there was a man who invested heavily when Bill Gates
started Microsoft and he became a multi-billionaire.
Looking at a picture of Bill and his wife, Melinda
both had pale indoor faces spending their time writing
checks to Africa.
The rich man decided to become a farmer of the old school
but since also remembered muddy boots from his childhood,
he made a mechanical, a big horse that could plough
six furrows at a time all he had to do, was to sit in a corner
and direct the horse which when coming to the end of a field
turned and ploughed in the opposite direction.
One day he forgot the on and off button and the horse
continued over total road destruction, and into a nearby
housing estate creating mayhem.
The rich man quickly had to rebuild and compensate his
shocked neighbours.
But people didn´t want the bloody wonder horse an
at a town hall meeting, he was banned from using it except
for an exhibition on how to be a modern farmer

the big lie

I surprise me the wrong choices we make to stake
our living in the tourist industry which has no future
and consist of bringing some people from a to b,
instead of farming and smaller industry
I rather make holes in a horseshoe than being
an airline pilot, this useless occupation I can
think of.
We have sent our viable industry to China and
created hole for ourselves so the bosses can make
a few pounds more it is tragic our shortcomings,we
have been side blinded by false promises and we walk
to the precipice for a day in the sun.
we have been hoodwinked into thinking a holiday is a human
right it is not, but work is, then a holiday nearby.

The end of an affair

a long maybe ten years relation with poem site
it has got a new editor who is critical of my work
finds it too brutal, left-wing and not sweet.
My work is being blocked out, and this is sad as there
is no point sending in poems that are no published?
Everything must come to, and end ends in death or
divorce, pity I have many friends there
and are used to send poetry a day.
Yes, my work is not for the faint heart it is about
a truth no one likes to hear.
I have though the content mattered
and it up to the reader to decide
So Farewell I will not be sending any work to
"Write out Loud"